📷 Table of Contents

Tools for Real Estate Do-ers
The Outline to Take You From Dreaming to Doing
By Amanda, *The Marketing Mama*

👍 Let My Life's Work WORK for You
📱 Visit www.YourMarketingMama.com
🎥 Subscribe to The Crazy Agent Dinner Party Show
📕 Grab the full Smart Agent Daily Planner on Amazon

Dreaming to doing. Consistently & constantly now for two decades.

I've been in the real estate game for over 20 years. Two solid decades of hustle, heartbreak, high-fives at closing, and yes, even the 2AM anxiety spirals wondering if I'll ever get another lead again. I really do love this industry—it's all I've ever known. And I've walked in every single pair of shoes you can wear in the real estate industry: buyer agent, solo agent, rain making team leader, boutique broker-owner, managing franchise broker, marketing mama, mortgage mama/lender, vital title owner, mentor, coach, burnt-out dreamer, and fired-up do-er.

Here's what I know for sure: we're not just agents—we're entrepreneurs. Self-employed. Self-made. No salary. No safety net. All-in.

If we were opening a pizza shop (stay with me), we wouldn't just hang a sign and start tossing dough—we'd know exactly what it takes to keep the lights on, right? Real estate is no different. This business requires tools, systems, and—most importantly—clarity.
You don't wing success. You build it.

You are your business. Not your broker. Not your team. Not your coach. Not your hilarious, fun-sized mentor (hi, that's me). YOU.
If you're not making intentional decisions about your career, your dream doesn't just stall—it slowly fades. And listen… we're in the business of making dreams come true. So let's make sure your dream doesn't die while you're out helping everyone else live theirs.
We are L-I-V-I-N, baby. And this workbook? It's your blueprint to go from dreaming to DO-ing.

I'm Amanda, *The Marketing Mama™* for #AllThingsRealEstate and in this workbook I've compiled my **Top 10 Tools for Real Estate Do-ers**—the same tools I've used and taught to help agents at every level design a real business with real direction. This isn't fluff. It's not a pep talk. It's the system that turns chaos into clarity, and intention into income.

Now that we've got our mindset straight, it's time to open the toolbox!

Agent Budget Builder

Your first step from "hoping for a closing" to running your biz like a boss.

Ah yes, commission-only income—the double-edged sword of the real estate world. On one side: freedom, unlimited potential, and that electric buzz that anything is possible. On the other side? A white-knuckle ride of feast-or-famine months where you seriously consider selling your socks—or worse, your soul—on OnlyFans.

If just thinking about relying on commissions makes you sweat through your blazer, you're not alone. But I've got you. The secret to surviving (and thriving) in this career isn't luck, it's planning. What better way to plan then a planner? If you don't have a planner you love, I'll humbly recommend mine: the **Smart Agent Daily Planner**, available on Amazon. It's got all 10 of these tools and so many more. But, friend to friend, before you spend money on anything, even my amazing and PROVEN planner, you MUST start with this first tool: The **Agent Budget Builder.**

Why this tool matters (like, a lot): I've closed thousands of transactions over the past 20+ years. You know what never gets less painful? Watching agents melt down mid-deal because they've got $18.26 in their bank account, no reserve fund, and someone in their life whispering "maybe you should get a real job" in their ear. It's a tale as old as time and I used to wonder how so many smart, hardworking people were always one surprise bill away from quitting…until I started mentoring agents back in 2006. And boom—there it was. Most agents don't budget. Like, at all.

This tool is your cure for that chaos. Because remember: you are your business. Not your broker, or your fun-sized mentor (hi again 👋). YOU. Remember, if you were opening a pizza shop, you'd know how much dough you needed (pun intended). So, let's fund it on purpose because **WE DON'T DO THIS FOR PRACTICE!**

■ How to Use the Agent Budget Builder - BE SPECIFIC

Let's start with the reality check: you need to know how much it costs you to exist each month—both personally and professionally. That means your housing expenses, vehicle expenses, cell phone bill, and more. But...get down to the nitty gritty. You need to add everything from your Netflix, Hulu, Disney+, all 12 subscriptions you forgot you had PLUS your weekly Olive Garden all-you-can-eat salad and breadsticks habit, etc.

Break. It. Down. Like a CPA with a grudge. ● Don't settle for vague categories like "utilities." And, if you've got a family depending on your income, include your expected contribution to their expenses too. My 8-year-old and 11-year-old both have phones, and yes, those line items are very real in my budget, because without Roblox I may not ever have finished this workbook for y'all! Bless. 🙏

One line item that I've seen trip up many an agent: GROCERIES. Don't skip this. You need fuel to function. My 17-year-old son eats like a linebacker. Our monthly food budget is basically a mortgage payment. So yes, line item everything from taco runs to date nights, from Botox to barbecues. Are you buying weekly scratch-offs? Tithing at church? If it's important to you and it makes you happy, it goes on here. There's nothing worse than seeing a sulking agent quit their dream because they failed to plan. Don't be one of the 87%*!

Same goes for business expenses. Be specific about marketing costs...if you've been donating a basket to the fundraiser at your kid's school, put it on here. Don't forget things like MLS dues, transaction fees, software, signage, lockboxes, client gifts, you name it. The reason this is important is you will want to eventually spend more money (we love shiny objects, don't we)...this will allow you to grow faster.

Yes, you will have some costs that go in both columns - your car expenses are different than your family's car expenses, your cell is separate from your family's in terms of business expenses. The goal is to know the totals of your personal expenses and your business expenses separately, and then also know the total of the two together.

● The Math That Matters

Once you've listed every expense, total your:
Personal monthly expenses _____

Business monthly expenses _____

Then, combine them for a grand total _____

Now take that total and multiply it by:

3 for your 3-month reserve baseline _____

6 for your ideal 6-month safety net _____

That final 3 or 6 month reserve number? That's how much you need saved to breathe easy while you build your real estate empire. That might mean keeping a side job, working on a team for a season, or getting creative with your savings.

I started with a 30% split under a seasoned agent—and still closed 50+ homes in my first year. You do what you need to do now, so your future self can do whatever the heck he/she/they wants later.👆

♟ Why This Tool Changes the Game
Most agents skip this. And that's exactly why most agents quit before they even get going. *87% leave the industry within the first 5 years.
This tool helps you:
Set realistic income goals
Take calculated risks
Make business decisions based on data, not panic
Be fully present for your clients
(instead of low-key stressing about gas money)

Your clients shouldn't have to suffer because you didn't plan. And neither should you. Build your business like a business. It starts here—with Tool #1: the **Agent Budget Builder**.
Let's get your pizza shop fully funded ▼.

AGENT BUDGET *Builder*

CHECK YO'SELF BEFORE YOU WRECK YO'SELF

Believe it or not, MANY Agents have zero idea what their budget is, & this is detrimental to their success, but also the success of your shared transactions. Don't be that Agent. You should know how much you NEED to make before setting the correct amount of time aside to accomplish this so you're not preoccupied with worry over your own finances when you're guiding your clients. Do the MATH so that you can take CALCULATED risks in your business, make decisions on data (not emotion), & be of the best service to your clients, your family, & most importantly, yourself.

MONTHLY PERSONAL

Home Payment
Home Insurance
Home Taxes
Home Maintenance
Car Payment/Transportation
Car Insurance
Car Maintenance
Power
Water/Sewer
Car Maintenance
Internet/TV
Family Obligations
Education
Groceries
Charity/Donations
Professional Services
Health/Medication
Self Care
Socialization/Lifestyle
Clothing
Credit Card Payments
Other Debt Payments
Travel
Other
Other
Other
Total Personal Expenses:

MONTHLY BUSINESS

Legal & License Fees
Association Dues
MLS Dues
Website & IDX Fees
CRM
Cell Phone
Print Marketing
Event Marketing
Online Marketing
Office Fees/Desk Fees
Broker/Transaction Fees
Client Credits
Client Gifts
Client Appreciation Events
E & O Insurance
eSignature/other Communication
Education Courses
Professional Development
Coaching & Subscriptions
Professional Counsel/Legal
Travel/Car Expenses
Other Software
Credit Card (Biz) Payments
Other Biz Debt Payments
Other
Other
Total Business Expenses:

3 MONTHS RESERVES

6 MONTHS RESERVES

One Page Business Plan

The most important math equation of your real estate life.

Let's get real for a sec—have you ever wanted to just quit real estate? Yeah…me too. But 20 years later, I'm still here. Stronger, smarter, and way more strategic. Because somewhere along the line, I realized the secret sauce was to stop winging it and start working a plan. And the simplest, most effective plan ever created?
Tool #2: the **One Page Business Plan**.

This tool is a total game changer. Whether you're brand new, burnt out, or somewhere in between, this one-page wonder gets you on track—or back on track—fast. Why? Because it doesn't just ask what you want to make… it shows you exactly what to do to get there.

⬤ Set Your GCI Goal (a.k.a. Your "Magic Number")

Let's start with what matters: your Gross Commission Income goal—the big, shiny number you want to hit for the year. But this isn't some "pick a number out of a hat" thing. You don't just say, "I want to make $100K" and hope the universe fills your inbox with leads. That's not how any of this works. This is math, not magic. ♟ You base your "want to" on your "got to," and then build from there.

So here's what you do:

✶ Take the annual total from Tool #1 (all your personal + business expenses, aka your "got to")

✶ Add a little cushion for growth, taxes, and your inevitable Olive Garden detours.

✶ Voilà—you've got your baseline GCI goal.

6

This **One Page Business Plan** will also account for your broker/team split, so you're not building castles in the sky—you're building based on reality. Now, it doesn't account for other variable expenses—but guess what? You've already listed those out in Tool #1. 👏

Pro tip: Don't wing your taxes either. If you don't know your bracket, don't just use that vague "20-30%" rule everyone tosses around. Get yourself an accountant. Someone you can add to your "gotta guy" list—aka your go-to team of professionals who know stuff you don't. Ideally, your new wing man for client referrals because *"Building Relationships That Build Business"* isn't just for clients—it's for your inner circle too.

📇 Backwards Math = Forward Progress

Here's the real juice of this **One Page Business Plan**: once you plug in your GCI goal, it reverse engineers your daily actions.
It tells you how many appointments you need to set.
It tells you how many calls you need to make.
It gives you a clear, do-able path to hit your number without guesswork or overwhelm.

Oh—and don't worry if numbers aren't your thing. The plan has simple instructions over each section. You won't get lost in the sauce. But if you do? Reach out. Come to Mama! I've got you, boo. All my contact info is on the last page of this little workbook.

🎩 Why This Tool Works

Most agents fail not because they're lazy, but because they lack clarity. This tool helps you turn "I need to make money" into "Here's exactly what I need to do today." Literally.

With the right mindset and systems, commission-only life goes from terrifying to thrilling. And, that's when the real magic happens.

The Marketing Mama's
AGENT ONE PAGE BUSINESS PLAN

AGENT NAME: DATE:

1. GROSS COMMISSION DESIRED	2. ACCOUNT FOR YOUR SPLIT
This is your total income before expenses	*Divide (1) by your commission split*

3. NEEDED SALES VOLUME	4. TRANSACTIONS NEEDED
Divide (2) by "standard" % commission	*Divide (3) by average sale price*

5. CALLS NEEDED EACH WEEK	6. APPTS NEEDED EACH WEEK
Divide (4) by YOUR conversion rate	*Divide (5) by 52 weeks*

WHERE IS YOUR BUSINESS COMING FROM?
- ☐ ....
- ☐ ....
- ☐ ....
- ☐ ....

LONG TERM GOALS
- ☐ ....
- ☐ ....
- ☐ ....
- ☐ ....

HOW MANY SOI ARE A SURE THING/REFERRERS? ....

DO YOU ALREADY HAVE A FARM AREA/NICHE? ....

@YOURMARKETINGMAMA

Millionaire Maker Checklist

The system that turns chaos into closings (& keeps you off the Hot Mess Express).

Let's do some quick math, shall we? Most agents spend about 2 hours a day just wondering what to do. Multiply that by 5 days a week, 52 weeks a year...and you get 520 hours. Divide that by 24 hours in a day, and boom—you've lost 21 full days a year just spinning your wheels.

That's three entire weeks of decision fatigue, second-guessing, and staring at your inbox like it holds the answers to the universe. (It doesn't. It holds 14 newsletters you forgot you subscribed to and a reminder that your lockbox battery is low.) Wouldn't you rather spend three weeks doing something fun? Enter Tool #3: the **Millionaire Maker Checklist**.
Your new daily GPS for staying out of chaos and in control.

⬢ Real Talk: Winging It Is Killing Your Business

There's no one right way to do real estate...but ohhh honey, there are a million wrong ones. And guess what's at the top of that list?
Winging it.

Winging it makes transactions messy, makes clients question your professionalism, and makes YOU spiral into *Chicken Little Syndrome*. You know the one: running around screaming "the sky is falling!" when really, you just forgot to confirm a showing and now everything feels like a crisis.

I created this tool to stop the spiral. This **Millionaire Maker Checklist**? It's your daily defense system. It's how you go from thinking "the sky is falling" to KNOWING the sky is the friggin' LIMIT! 🚀

The **Millionaire Maker Checklist** was the catalyst to my entire *Mama Machine Movement*. I talk about it often on my "real" Real Estate show, the **Crazy Agent Dinner Party**. If you've never seen my show, forgive yourself, but please, if you truly do want to sell more real estate and have way more fun doing it, go binge it ASAP...and please like and subscribe. We have a ton of fun on the show and I just love hosting it, because it's the living embodiment of my *Mama Machine Movement*...which is founded in the concept that closes deals: it's time to get REAL about Real Estate.

Real Estate IS Crazy! YES! But YOU don't have to be!👉💊.
In my opinion, one of the best ways to combat crazy? Systems. This **Millionaire Maker Checklist**? It's the foundation of my systems.
Systems > stress.

◼ Why It Works: Sexy? No. Necessary? OH YES.
This isn't some fluffy morning routine that requires lavender tea and sunrise journaling. (Though hey, if that's your thing, live your truth.)

The **Millionaire Maker Checklist** is made up of the not-so-sexy but oh-so-necessary daily habits that I've used across 5 career phases and 3 markets. It's the reason I've made a million dollars in the real estate industry time and again, and so many of my Realtor Partners have too.

Think of it as your daily revenue rhythm—a sequence of smart, strategic actions that keep you moving, building, and growing. Because let's face it: this business is HARD. You wear a thousand hats. You juggle lead gen, client care, contracts, admin, training, marketing, social media, and—oh yeah—your actual life.

So without a system? 👉 You spiral. 👉 You stall.
👉 You stay stuck in reaction mode.

But with a system? 👉 You soar. 🚀
10

The Marketing Mama's
MILLIONAIRE MAKER CHECKLIST
DAILY INSTRUCTIONS

1. Best Practice: print & tape to your workspace OR buy my **Smart Agent Daily Planner** on Amazon to have each day, week, & month mapped out for your success with over 180 pages, your year is covered for success!
2. Complete tasks & check them off the list. If you don't complete, don't check! Measuring accurately will keep you accountable & you need that DATA to deliver the RESULTS. Utilize 2 & New Tracker for prospecting notes.
3. Repeat these not-so-sexy but oh-so-necessary daily habits to sell more real estate (& have more fun).
4. Be kind to yourself...but also don't settle for excuses. Eat the Nutella out of the jar & then get to gettin'!
5. Start each working day with an INTENTIONAL EFFORT to be a PROFESSIONAL. Mornings should be steady & structured, gathering details & data to allow those afternoons/evenings/weekends, my Weekend Warriors, to be more flexible & fluid (without freaking out).
6. REMINDER! Always have a contingency plan mapped out. Working hours are hours for working. Stay on course.

POWERFUL PRODUCTION	**BEGIN, INTENTIONALLY**	Begin a daily habit of being intentional about your day. Whether it's exercise, meditation, affirmations, visualization, WHATEVER...get yourself geared up for greatness. POSITIVE THOUGHTS = POSITIVE RESULTS. NO DRAMA - love, Mama!
	HOW'S THE MARKET	This is MARKET specific research/data tracking to help you be of better service to your current clients and/or your desired farm area/niche. This is where HOT SHEETS help! Daily effort to be the expert results in regular OPPORTUNITIES to actually BE THE EXPERT. Educated answers when asked (and we're always asked) are the open door to start opening doors (get it, 'cause we sell houses). They also save deals. PERIOD.
	CURRENT CONTRACTS	Separate from the Weekly Updates to Buyer/Seller (below), this item is a daily reminder to address the dates/appointments/contingencies/fires/etc. of your current contracts. It's your job to see the contract through. It's your job to keep the contract together. It's your job to stay in compliance. And if you don't do your job, you don't get paid. Be poised & professional with a PLAN. Reminder, there's always going to be something that comes up because each contract has different people & different scenarios. So, while you won't know all the answers all the time, take the time to get the answers & provide the DATA TO DELIVER RESULTS. If you don't have current contracts, that's your cue for getting your mission critical prospects out of limbo & on with their life.
	CLIENTS IN QUEUE = AGENT CUE	This is line item specific to Buyers/Sellers who have agreed to work with you to buy/sell within 3 months. These MISSION CRITICAL clients are not yet pending sale or under contract. That's your CUE as an agent to fully understand their WHY, WHEN & HOW & make it your MISSION: OUT OF LIMBO, ON WITH LIFE!
	THE ORGANIZED AGENT	IF YOU DID IT, LOG IT. You will spend so much less time wondering what to do next if you know what you did last. Also use this time to prep for any appointments of the day/week ahead.
PURPOSEFUL PROSPECTING	**REHEARSAL/PRACTICE**	In SALES you perform at the level you practice. We are better prepared if we practice scripts with the right tone & canned responses. Be sure to practice the script for the type of prospecting you're doing on that day. KNOW YOUR AUDIENCE.
	2 - SOI/DATABASE	Connecting with clients you have sold real estate to & people you personally know needs to be part of your DAILY HABITS. You can't be a secret agent & make money.
	NEW LEADS/THE WHEN	Any referral you have received until communication reciprocates. And then any of the leads in your pipeline that are later than 3 months. THEIR WHEN IS YOUR WHEN.
	VIDEO CMA FOR THE WIN	This is your time to shine. Prospective Sellers who have pondered selling can get a lot of the answers they need from any old agent, but they don't want any old agent, they want and THEY NEED YOU! If you commit to doing 2 Video CMAs each week & combine it with dropping off your Active Marketing Plan-WOWSA!
BOTH	**SHOWTIME/GAME ON**	ACTUAL APPOINTMENTS: Showings & Listings Presentations. BRING IT!
	POST SHOW/GAME RECAP	Do the whole job so you can have a whole LIFE. Do an in the moment recap so you can sharpen your skills, communicate effectively, & WIN/WOW EVERY TIME!

The Marketing Mama's
MILLIONAIRE MAKER CHECKLIST WEEK OF: _____

M T W R F S S   DAILY

- Begin, INTENTIONALLY
- How's the Market
- Current Contracts
- Clients in Queue = Agent Cue
- The Organized Agent
- Rehearsal/Practicing
- 2 - SOI/Database
- ALL "New" Leads/"The When"
- Video CMA for the Win
- Showtime/Game On
- Post Show/Game Recap

WEEKLY

- Expert Agent Training
- Accountability Meeting
- Weekly Update: Buyers
- Weekly Update: Sellers
- Smart Agent Time
- Re-Evaluate Client "Why"
- Community Involvement
- Industry Involvement
- Social Media Post - 1
- Social Media Post - 2
- Track Income/Expenses

GCI Goal: $_____/YTD GCI: $_____

____ Transactions @ ____Conv Rate = ____Calls ____ Appts

NOTES:

Monday:

Tuesday:

Wednesday:

Thursday:

Friday:

Saturday:

Sunday:

New Leads/When

Any referral you have received in the last 24-hrs; until communication reciprocates

"The When" - 3-6 mos

"The When" - 6 mos+/Pillar

Current Clients

Mission Critical = 1-3 mos Buyers/Sellers: get out of limbo on on with life!

WHY, WHEN, HOW?

Hot Buyers (POF/PA)

Warm Buyers (PQ)

Sellers & Potential Sellers

2 - SOI/Database

Clients you've sold real estate to or have worked with; people you know. Don't be a secret agent!

10 SOI Contacted

10 SOI Results

🏆 WINS:

Realtor Rules For Business

Stop waiting for people to take your job seriously—and start showing them how.

Here's the weirdest thing that happens the moment you get your real estate license: you become a millionaire with nothing but free time. ●
At least, that's what everyone around you seems to think.
Suddenly, your time is public domain. You're "available" for errands, school pick-ups, mid-morning vent sessions, or clearing out Aunt Susan's garage... because hey, you don't have a real job, right?

Wrong.
Real estate is a real job.
And Tool #4: **Real Job Rules** is how you start treating it like one.

● Reality Check: If You Don't Set Boundaries, No One Will

Maybe you wanted the flexibility that comes with this business—but here's the hard truth: You'll never have that freedom unless you set rules that align with your goals, and communicate those rules with the people who matter most in your life.

And I mean real rules. Not vague intentions. RULES.
Expectations. Structure. Boundaries. That's what this tool delivers.

Every traditional job has a workplace manual. Policies. Procedures. Guidelines. But in real estate? You're the HR department, the CEO, and the front desk receptionist.

So it's time to write your own rules.

14

💬 The Conversation That Changed Everything

Let me tell you a story. It was 2007. I was pregnant with my first son, leading a growing team, chasing a huge GCI goal, and trying to plan my maternity leave like a sane, responsible businesswoman.

But one day, my mom—who's a cardiac ICU nurse—got visibly upset when I couldn't talk to her on the phone for hours like we used to. I told her: "Mom, if I called you while someone was coding, I wouldn't be mad if you said you couldn't talk—you're literally saving lives. I've got lives in my hands too. And one growing in my belly."
(She reminded me it was my uterus, not my belly, because moms.)
But that moment? It hit different. She finally saw that just because I didn't clock into a hospital didn't mean I wasn't carrying the weight of real responsibilities. And it forced me to recognize something too:
If you don't take your real estate job seriously, no one else will.

🔶 Build the Foundation: Define Your Rules
You've already done the hard math (Tool #1), set the income goal (Tool #2), and built the daily system (Tool #3). Now? It's time to build your business boundaries.

Start by setting your own "**Real Job Rules.**"

<u>Here are a few to consider:</u>
No personal calls until prospecting goals are met
No scrolling until checklist is complete
Working hours: *[insert your business hours here]*
Days off: *[insert your actual rest days]*
Emergency protocol: Who handles what when life goes sideways? (You know, like when the dog eats something sketchy, or you're out of milk, or the school calls you again.)

This might sound rigid, but it's not about being inflexible—it's about being intentional. And hey, if your partner has a "real job" with rules and expectations, then so do you.

Be clear. Be confident. Be fair. (**Pro tip:** Go into the convo with a compromise already in mind—like swapping school pick-up shifts.)

● Why This Tool Matters

Without rules, your business becomes a source of burnout—not freedom. Without expectations, you feel like you're always working but never getting anywhere. Without boundaries, people (even the well-meaning ones) unintentionally undermine your efforts. And that little voice in your head that whispers "you're not doing enough"? It gets louder every time you miss a goal or skip a task for someone else's "just one thing."

But when you define and enforce your own carefully curated **Real Job Rules**, everything shifts:
You earn respect—from others and from yourself.
You stop justifying your work—and start owning it.
You become the boss of your business—not just in title, but in mindset.

▰ This Is the Line in the Sand
You are building a business.
You are making real money moves.
You are creating a life of purpose and possibility.

And none of that happens by chance.

So if you're tired of feeling stretched thin, unsupported, or unseen—start here. Write your rules. Post them. Share them. Live them.
Because the world won't treat real estate like a real job... until you do.
And baby, you're a **Real Estate Do-er** now. Time to act like it. ◀✦

RULES FOR *Business*

Even though you're a person, you're also a **BUSINESS**. You defined **GOALS** to keep you, aka **THE BUSINESS**, functioning. Now, lay out some ground **RULES** for your business. **RULES** are different than **GOALS**, but they are essential to keep you on track for those goals. **PRO TIP RULE**: No personal calls until all tasks are done for the day.

1	
2	
3	
4	
5	
6	
7	
8	

Now it's time to **SET EXPECTATIONS** with the support people in your life.
Sign off on the expectation so now you both acknowledge the **RULES**!

Supporter Name _____   Date Expectations Set _____

Agent Signed _____   Supporter Signed _____

@YOURMARKETINGMAMA

Agent Marketing Wheel

What gets tracked gets traction. And gets traction gets closings (and confidence).

Let's be honest: you can't always control how many homes you sell this month. But you can control where your time, energy, and money go.

That's where Tool #5 comes in—the **Agent Marketing Wheel**.

Because if marketing is the engine of your business, this is the diagnostic tool that keeps you from burning out—or stalling out—on the side of the road. It's literally the wheel that keeps you moving.

⬤ Marketing = Movement

The most important job you have in real estate isn't writing contracts or showing homes—it's marketing. Where you market is where you will receive leads from. This is called a lead source.

Marketing is the center of real estate, hence my moniker, "***The Marketing Mama***," given to me by my mentor, Robert Palmer, CEO of LPT Realty. So, marketing must be the central focus of your business.
It's the wheel that keeps you moving.

No marketing? No movement. Period.

Every lead source you use is a spoke on that **Agent Marketing Wheel**—and if you don't know which ones are working, which ones are draining you, and which ones bring you joy, you're not running a business...
you're running in circles.

18

⚒ How the Agent Marketing Wheel Works

This super simple tool helps you track your lead sources, identify which ones are producing actual deals, spot where you're spending your time & money, and decide what to double down on—or let go of.

Here's how to use it:

1. In each spoke, list one of your marketing lead sources.
2. In the "DEALS" box, record how many closed, pending, or active transactions came from each source.
3. In the blank space beside it, list how many total leads you received from that lead source—even if they didn't convert. Because here's the truth: if a source isn't turning into business, you need to evaluate why. Maybe the problem isn't the source—it's your follow-up, timing, or communication.

That's not a failure. That's feedback. 🔍

Need help thinking of lead sources? Here's some common lead sources to get you rolling: SOI/Sphere Referrals, Agent/Team Referrals, Open Houses, Farming, Online Leads, FSBO/Expired, Door Knocking, Social Media, Direct Mail, BNI, Church, PTA, etc —anything that touches people and produces potential leads.

⬛ ROI vs. ROH (Return on Happiness)

Here's the part most coaches won't tell you:
Not every winning marketing source is going to be about money.
Some of your lead sources may not yet have produced a closing—but they might still be worth it. Why?
Because they make you happy.
Because they connect you to your community.
Because when people think real estate, they think you.

And in this business, that's a HUGE win.

Example: Let's say you sit on your kid's PTA board. You've gotten a few leads but no closings yet. Should you ditch it? Not necessarily. If it fills your bucket and reminds people you're their go-to agent, that's a marketing win, and those seeds often bloom when you least expect it.

🪣 But... If It's Draining You? BYE.

Use this tool to focus on how you get leads. If a marketing lead source:
Doesn't make you money
AND
Doesn't make you happy
Then guess what? It's time to pivot. We call that dead weight.

And Do-ers? We don't carry dead weight into our next season. 🎉

The **Agent Marketing Wheel** gives you clarity. And clarity gives you confidence. No boss? No problem. This is how you hold yourself accountable—with love, strategy, and data.

♥ Final Thought: Time Is the Currency of Your Life

Every task you do today is a trade. You're exchanging one day of your life for it. So if you're going to spend your time marketing—you better make sure it's worth it.

If it gets results? Keep it.

If it brings joy? Nurture it.

If it does neither? Shake it off, shake it up, and MOVE ON.

You're not just building a business—you're building a life.

And Tool #5 will help make sure both are aligned, intentional, and absolutely unstoppable.

20

AGENT MARKETING *Wheel*

You can't always control the volume in sales, but you can control what you spend money & time on. Marketing is the center of your business…it's the wheel that keeps you moving. You should have many marketing/lead sources. If a source you've spent time or money on isn't producing results: **PIVOT.**

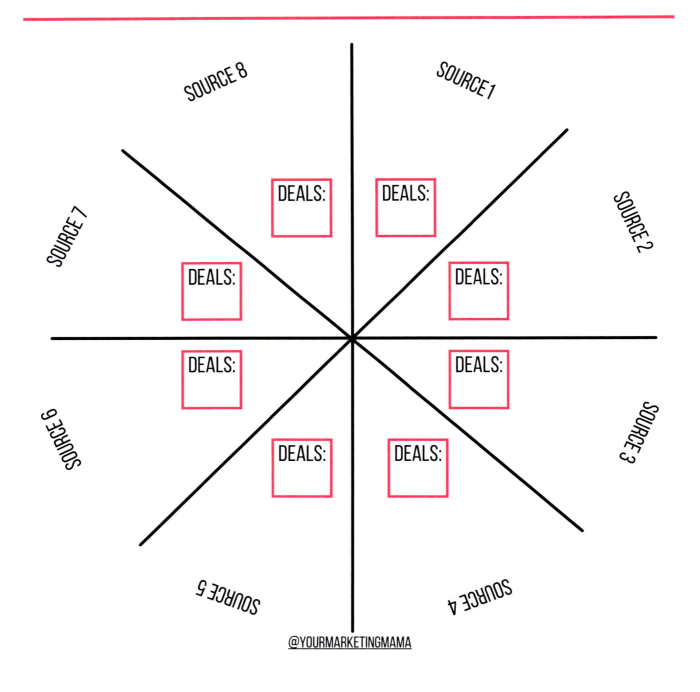

EXPENSE TRACKER

Agent Expense Tracker

Check yo'self before you wreck yo'self—financially, emotionally, & professionally.

Let me ask you something:

Have you ever had a deal with an emotional agent?

Worse… have you ever been the emotional agent?

Yeah. It happens. And 9 times out of 10, that meltdown didn't come from the paperwork—it came from pressure. Financial pressure. Because when money gets tight, people stop making smart decisions and start making emotional ones.

And that's bad for everyone in the deal.

It's Not Just About Money—It's About Mental Stability

As we covered in Tool #1 (Agent Budget Builder), too many agents have no clue what it actually costs to run their business. And without that awareness, they're constantly on edge, unknowingly putting their clients —and their own success—at risk.

Because here's what I've learned over thousands of transactions and two decades in this business:

Your clients will often take on the personality of the craziest person in the transaction. And if that person is you…? Baby, we've got a problem.

That's why Tool #6: the **Agent Expense Tracker** is so crucial.

The Tracker That Keeps You Sane (and Solvent)

Your Agent Marketing Wheel (Tool #5) is what keeps the wheel spinning… This tool? It's the ride-or-die that tells you whether the Marketing Wheel's getting you anywhere.

Use this tool to track:

🏷️Every business expense

🏷️Relevant personal expenses

💰Closings in the hopper

And, it should be a glaring reminder to cross-reference your lead sources with actual results because, as DJ Quik once said:

"If it don't make dollars, it don't make sense." 💃🔲

This tracker gives you that clarity. It's how you turn hustle into results—and stress into systems.

📓 Pro Tip: Make Admin Days Your Business Self-Care

Here's the deal: Agents constantly tell me they "don't have time to track."

But let's do the math.

There are 168 hours in a week. If you don't spend at least one of them measuring your money, you're trading 168 hours for zero accountability— week after week after week.

Success or excuses—you only get to pick one.

So here's what I recommend:

👉 Take ONE hour a week to update your expenses.

👉 At a bare minimum, dedicate ONE admin day per month to review your expenses, recalculate your ROI, clean up your systems, check your mindset, and level up.

That's not boring—it's self-care for your business.

Friend, you are the business. And no one else is going to manage your money for you—unless you've earned the right to outsource it by actually growing something worth managing.

■ A Few Expense-Tracking Tips (From the Crunchwrap Queen Herself)
If you've never tracked your business expenses before, start simple:
1. Use a dedicated business bank account or credit card. Mixing personal and business expenses? Total chaos.
2. Download your monthly transactions as a CSV file. Sort by vendor. You'll quickly see if you've been spending $200 a month on apps you don't even remember downloading.
3. Look for patterns. Are you paying monthly for tools you could save money on by switching to an annual plan (hello, Follow Up Boss, Dropbox, Canva Pro)? That's real savings.

And yes...tracking spending helped break my Crunchwrap Supreme habit. (RIP, cheesy addiction. You were delicious. You were expensive.)

♥ You're Not Just Spending Money—You're Building a Business
Remember: you are helping people make one of the biggest purchases of their lives.
That comes with responsibility.
It also comes with opportunity.
But you cannot grow what you don't measure. You can't scale what you don't track.
Tracking your expenses might not be glamorous.
It won't make you go viral on Instagram.
And no one's sending you commission checks just for doing it.
But it's the backbone of a healthy, sustainable, scalable business.
And yes—I'm giving you these tools because I want you to buy my planner, join my membership, and watch the show. But more than that, I want to see this industry change. I want YOU to sell more real estate and have way more fun doing it.

● Final Word: You Are Not Just a Self. You Are a Business.
Start treating yourself like one.

The Marketing Mama's
AGENT EXPENSE TRACKER

MONTH:

INCOME

DESCRIPTION	GROSS AMOUNT	AFTER TAX
CLOSING 1:		
CLOSING 2:		
OTHER: :		
TOTAL		

FIXED EXPENSES

DATE	DESCRIPTION	AMOUNT
	TOTAL	

VARIABLE EXPENSES

DATE	DESCRIPTION	AMOUNT
	TOTAL	

	BUDGET	ACTUAL	DIFFERENCE
TOTAL INCOME			
TOTAL EXPENSES			
TOTAL SAVINGS			
DEBT PAYOFF			
NET BALANCE			

NOTES:

@YOURMARKETINGMAMA

Lessons & Blessings Review

Because what doesn't kill you makes you...a better agent (and a stronger human).

Let's get something straight:
Real estate is not for the faint of heart.
Some days, you're poppin' champagne after a closing. Other days, you're dragging soggy open house signs in the rain, wondering if you've somehow been cast in a hidden-camera show called "Will This Deal Ever Happen?" It's a rollercoaster.
Highs, lows, and plenty of "meh" in between. But here's the truth that keeps real estate pros sane:
Every moment is either a lesson or a blessing.
Every setback, every win—it's shaping you.

Tool #7, the **Lessons & Blessings Review**, is your space to seriously pause, process, and power up.

◼ Why This Tool Matters (More Than You Think)

Reflection isn't fluff. It's not woo-woo or warm-and-fuzzy journaling.
It's data with heart. And in this business? You need both.
I've worked with hundreds of agents, and I can tell you this:
The ones who grow the most are the ones who stop and learn the most.
Reflection sharpens your self-awareness
It makes you a better decision-maker
It gives you grace—and grit—on hard days
And it helps you stay grounded when the chaos comes
(and oh, it will come)…

✦ Step 1: Celebrate the Blessings

Start with the good stuff. The wins. The moments that made you proud.
The proof that your work is working.
Not every blessing is a closing. In fact, most aren't.
Some are subtle. Quiet. Unseen by the world—but so very important to
your journey.
What counts as a blessing? Here's some examples:
A new listing or referral (yes!)
A sweet review from a client—even if the deal didn't close
Mastering a skill: objections, negotiation, or finally not panicking during that
Instagram reel
A lead texts you back after weeks of silence and says, "Thanks for following up—I'll
call you when we're ready."

That's momentum. That's planting seeds. That's the business becoming real.
The more you notice and celebrate your blessings, the easier it gets to
keep going when the grind gets tough.

● Step 2: Own the Lessons

Now comes the truth-telling part.
Look at the things that didn't go so hot. Not to shame yourself—but to
refine yourself. Practice saying, "I never fail. I only learn."
What counts as a lesson? Here's some examples:
A deal falls through. Oof. A client ghosts you. Shocker.
You host an open house and no one shows up. (Except you...and a tray of cookies.)
You miss your prospecting goals. Again.
You buy the shiny new lead system...and never log in.

Ask yourself: What went wrong? Was it in my control? What can I do
differently next time? Lessons are your growth points.
They're not setbacks—they're setups.
But only if you're brave enough to name them. Include both business and
personal blessings and lessons for true, constant growth.

27

● Real Talk: Reflection Builds Resilience

As an entrepreneur, your brain is juggling a million tabs at once. Showings, follow-ups, content, contracts… no wonder you're exhausted.

Reflection is what helps you:

◼ See the patterns in your progress
◼ Catch what's working (and do more of it)
◼ Release what's not working (and do less of it)
◼ Protect your peace while still chasing your potential

▥ How to Use This Tool

At the end of each month:
Block off ONE HOUR MINIMUM.
Turn off your phone or put on DND.
Do NOT check your emails.
No distractions. No multitasking. Just you, your thoughts, and this tool.

List your blessings.

The wins. The growth. The moments that matter.

List your lessons.

Get honest. Get curious. Not cruel—curious.

Extract the wisdom.

Ask: What does this teach me about how I do business, how I manage stress, or how I need to pivot next month?

This is your monthly mindset reset.
Your check-in with your future CEO self.
Hear me now—it's self-care for your spirit
and strategic maintenance for your long-term success.

💬 My Real-Life Example: Avoiding Means No Advancing

There was a time recently I avoided this tool completely.
Because facing the truth hurt.
I was grieving. I was overwhelmed. I was humiliated by a season I didn't
ask for. And instead of processing the pain—I powered through.
Big mistake.

Avoiding reflection didn't protect me.
It paralyzed me. I was stuck. And the spiral?
Was real.

But when I started using this **Lessons & Blessings Review** again
I started to heal.
Personally. Professionally. Financially. Emotionally. Spiritually.

So when I tell you this tool matters? I'm not talking theory.
I'm talking survival. I'm talking growth. I'm talking peace.

■ Final Thought: You're Human First, Agent Second

Let's not forget:
You're allowed to feel.
You're allowed to fall apart sometimes.
You're allowed to pivot when something isn't working.
This tool gives you permission to do all of that—without losing your way.
Because the goal isn't perfection.
It's progress.
And real estate? It's not a sprint—it's a soul marathon.
With zigs and zags, and sometimes, setbacks. But also with so much joy.

So pause. Reflect. Review. Accept your lessons. Celebrate your blessings.
And then… get back to doing what you do best:
building a beautiful business and life.

MONTH OF:

The Marketing Mama's
LESSONS & BLESSINGS REVIEW

GOAL: _____

START DATE :   DUE DATE :

NOTES & HAPPENINGS:

LESSONS:

BLESSINGS:

Monthly Measures

Because feelings don't pay the bills—results do.

I hate to break it to you, but no one's cashing checks based on how "busy" you feel. Feelings don't pay your bills—results do. And how do you get consistent results? Easy:

Plan the work. Work the plan. Measure the data. Make intentional changes. Rinse and repeat.

If I asked you right now, "Hey, **Real Estate Dreamer**… how's business going?" — would you have a confident answer?

If your response is anything between "uhhhh" and "I think okay?" — then you're in the right place.

Tool #8: **Monthly Measures** is your permission slip to stop guessing and start knowing.

■ Why Measuring Matters More Than Motivation

Here's what I know: I LOVE data.

I nerd out on numbers and I don't care who knows! But I don't love data just for fun—I love it because data is the secret to long-term, bank-account-busting success in real estate.

If you can't measure your business, you can't manage your business. And if you can't manage it, you're stuck winging it. And you know how I feel about winging it…🐔🐓

Mama Machine Methodology: Plan. Track. Analyze. Adjust.

This tool ties it all together. It's your monthly pulse check to stop you from ending up on the "just barely getting by" hamster wheel of doom.

💡 Predictable Results > Real Estate Chaos

Let me ask you a another question:

Are the hours, energy, and dollars you're pouring into your business actually paying off?

If you don't know...how can you fix it?

How can you grow it?

You can't.

That's why Tool #8 exists—to shine a spotlight on what's really working... and what's just keeping you busy.

Because the goal here isn't just more hustle—it's SMART hustle.

This tool helps you:

Track key performance metrics every month

Monitor your conversion rates

Assess the effectiveness of your marketing

Identify what's gaining traction—and what's costing you time and money

🔍 Let's Talk Conversion Rate (Don't Skip This)

Here's a fun experiment I run with every agent I've ever coached:

"What's your conversion rate from your sphere of influence?"

And the two most common answers are:

1. "I don't know."

2. "100%" (spoiler alert...no, it's not)

Then five minutes later, they're telling me how their cousin just bought a house with someone else. 🔔

Let's prevent that.

If you're using these tools, you'll be tracking your contacts, calls, appointments, offers, and closed deals... and measuring them month over month. That means you'll know:

Where your leads are coming from

How well you're converting them

Where you're leaking time, energy, and revenue

And best of all? You'll have data to guide your decisions. Not just vibes. Because as a self-employed, commission-only income sales person, vibes and feelings usually don't matter with the matter at hand.

This tool is your vibe curator to focus those feelings.
It gives you the skills that pay the bills. Actually.
All by MEASURING.

● Start Thinking Like a CEO, Not a Salesperson
If you want predictable income in this unpredictable industry, Tool #8 is your path to stability and growth.

Track the right numbers consistently, and guess what...
You know when to invest more.
You know what to cut.
You know which strategies are working.
And you stop taking every dry month personally, because now you've got the data to pivot with power.

■ Final Thought: Dream About It or Be About It
At this point, you've got the tools:
A budget and a business plan ■
A daily checklist ■
A real job mindset ■
A marketing system ■
A reflection ritual ■
Now it's time to track your performance.
Not to prove anything to anyone else—but to prove to yourself that you're doing the work and it's working. Because success in this business?
It doesn't come from luck. It comes from intention.
So ask yourself: Are you gonna keep dreaming about success—or are you gonna start being about it?

IF IT DON'T MAKE DOLLARS, IT DON'T MAKE SENSE.

If you don't **MEASURE** it, you can't **MANAGE** it. Plus, feelings don't pay your bills, **RESULTS** do. This year you're committed to live your Real Estate life by **DESIGN**, not default. Tracking your progress will help you to stay on course & make best use of your time.

WIN THE NUMBERS GAME BY TRACKING

◯	◯	◯
TOTAL HOURS PROSPECTING	TOTAL SHOWINGS OR CONSULTATIONS SET	TOTAL NEW ACTIVE BUYERS
◯	◯	◯
TOTAL NEW LISTING PROSPECTS	TOTAL LISTING APPOINTMENTS	TOTAL LISTINGS TAKEN

CONVERSION CHECK -UP

◯ TOTAL APPOINTMENTS ÷ ◯ TOTAL CALLS MADE = ◯ CALL CONVERSION RATIO

◯ TOTAL NEW ACTIVE BUYERS ÷ ◯ TOTAL SHOWING OR CONSUTLATIONS = ◯ BUYER CONVERSION RATIO

◯ TOTAL LISTING APPOINTMENTS ÷ ◯ TOTAL LISTINGS TAKEN = ◯ LISTING CONVERSION RATIO

Quarterly Goal Tracker

Because success isn't magic—it's math. With a side of strategy.

Let me ask you:

Are you a spaghetti noodle agent?

Just throwin' stuff at the wall to see what sticks? ●

I mean, don't get me wrong—I love a good plate of carbs, but when it comes to building a profitable, sustainable real estate business, wingin' it is not the vibe, remember?

The agents who win in this business aren't just "working hard"—they're working SMART, using data to drive decisions and strategy to drive growth.

That's where Tool #9—the **Quarterly Goal Tracker**—comes in.
It's how we stop guessing and start growing.

● Why Quarterly Tracking is a Game-Changer

Let's get one thing straight: real estate is cyclical and seasonal.
One month can be slow, the next a sprint. If you're only looking at monthly numbers, you're seeing the forest through a straw.

Quarterly tracking smooths out the rollercoaster and helps you:
●●Spot trends
●Course correct in real-time

See real progress without overreacting to a slow week or a little dry spell.
Think of this tool like your business's weather radar. It helps you forecast, prepare, and adjust your plan before the storm hits—or celebrate that sunshine when things click.

35

■ Data Isn't Just Numbers—It's Your Roadmap

If you follow me, you know I say this all the time:

"Data delivers results"

But let's unpack that. Because data isn't just a bunch of boring numbers on a spreadsheet—it's a direction to drive you.

When you consistently track your Key Performance Indicators (KPIs), you're not just collecting info. You're:

Identifying what's working ■
Spotting what's not ●
Making smarter decisions 🚀
Staying motivated by visible progress ✴

And here's the best part: with every quarter you track, your confidence builds. You're no longer hoping it works—you're watching it work.

💼 What Are You Tracking Exactly?

Your KPIs are the data points we've already laid out using Tools 1–8.
Quick recap:
Tool #1: Your personal + business budget defined💰
Tool #2: Your GCI goal (based on what you need to live + thrive) ⬤
Tool #3: Your daily + weekly tasks to hit those goals ■
Tool #4: Your rules for work/life boundaries ⏰
Tool #5: Your marketing lead sources 🌐
Tool #6: Your actual expenses 🐢
Tool #7: Your wins and losses 🛐
Tool #8: Your conversion rate calculator 🗒

■Now, Tool #9 helps you take all that and zoom out.

You're looking at your progress quarter by quarter to see how consistent effort stacks into serious results.

■ Real Estate Is a Roller Coaster. This Tool Is the Seatbelt.
If you've been in the game for more than five minutes, you know:
One amazing month can be followed by crickets.
That's not failure.
That's normal "real life" real estate.

But that's also why you need this tool, the **Quarterly Goal Tracker**. It:
Adjusts for market shifts (seasonality, rates, buyer behavior)
Helps you avoid reactionary panic mode
Creates a record of what's working so you can double down
Because a slow January could be offset by a booming March—but you won't know unless you zoom out and look at the big picture.

✹ When It Clicks, It Really Clicks
There is nothing—and I mean nothing—more satisfying than seeing how your consistency has paid off in black-and-white numbers. ■
You defined your goals up front. You stuck to your plan (or adjusted it). You watched your YTD numbers grow quarter after quarter.
When my Realtor partners hit me up to share their wins, it's not always about the number of homes they sold.
It's that lightbulb moment when they realize:
"Wait... this actually works. I'm not guessing anymore. I'm growing now."
And THAT right there? **That's my why.** 🕯🔥

◼ Final Word: Dreamers Dream. Do-ers Do. Data Delivers.
You can hustle hard and still feel stuck if you don't pause to track what's happening.
You're building a business, not just working a job.
You're aiming for profitability, not just activity.
You want predictable growth, not just accidental wins.
So, ask yourself:
Are you still throwing spaghetti? Or are you building a sustainable business?

The Marketing Mama's
QUARTERLY GOAL TRACKER

QUARTER:

AIN'T NOTHIN' WRONG WITH BEING A GOAL DIGGER

Time to see if your year-to-date **PROGRESS** measures up with your annual goals you are committed to achieving! If it doesn't? Time to **DECONSTRUCT** to **DOMINATE**!

GOALS VS. CURRENT

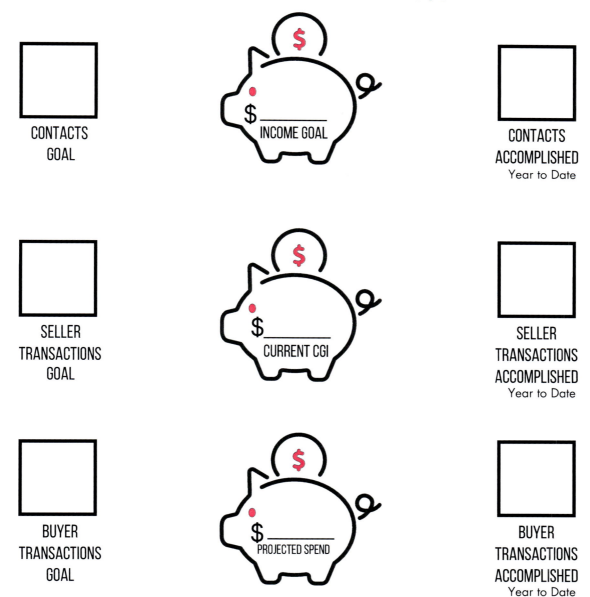

CONTACTS GOAL

$ _____ INCOME GOAL

CONTACTS ACCOMPLISHED
Year to Date

SELLER TRANSACTIONS GOAL

$ _____ CURRENT CGI

SELLER TRANSACTIONS ACCOMPLISHED
Year to Date

BUYER TRANSACTIONS GOAL

$ _____ PROJECTED SPEND

BUYER TRANSACTIONS ACCOMPLISHED
Year to Date

@YOURMARKETINGMAMA

Agent Contingency Plan

Because even when your client ghosts, your goals shouldn't.

Let's start with a simple truth that may shock you:

There. 💥 Are. 💥 No. 💥 Real. 💥 Estate. 💥 Emergencies. 💥

Okay, okay… I'll admit, on the very first episode of the ***Crazy Agent Dinner Party***, we did feature a screenshot of one of my agent's cars LITERALLY ON FIRE on the way to a home inspection.

That was an emergency. 🔥🚗

But most things? Not so much.

As I've mentioned before in this workbook, and say nearly on repeat: real estate, by its very nature, is a perpetual series of tiny catastrophes. And if you don't have systems in place, those little crises can make you spiral.

I created Tool #10: **The Contingency Plan** because sometimes you don't need to "figure it out." Sometimes, you just need a plan B that doesn't involve crying in your car.

👻 Let's Talk About Ghosting

What's one of the most common catastrophes agents face?

Getting ghosted.

The buyer flakes. The seller cancels. The "urgent" Zillow lead who must see the house tonight never shows up. You rearranged your life, sacrificed family time, skipped dinner—and then poof. Nothing.

Cue the spiral (and the alcohol).

But listen up: ghosting is not a personal attack—it's a business reality and when things are out of your control, you must take control of yourself.

39

● This Is Why You Need a Contingency Plan

The Contingency Plan is a simple system you can deploy immediately when someone ghosts, cancels, or pulls the old "radio silence."
Instead of letting your emotions hijack the moment:
You redirect the time toward meaningful work
You preserve your confidence
You take action (not things personally)

Think of it like this: You blocked time for business.
Someone else bailed. You don't bail on yourself.
Use that time to invest in you.

■ What Goes in the Plan?

Start by making a list of all the things you've been meaning to learn, clean up, or set up in your business. It could include:
Learning how to create a hot sheet in your MLS
Updating your CRM templates
Mastering that neighborhood farming strategy
Researching new tools or training videos
Creating a new social media series

But! Here's the game changer, here's what takes it from a list to a living, breathing ACTUAL Contingency Plan that you can put into action quickly:
Next to each item on the list add the link, app, login, or class info you'll need to actually do it, IMMEDIATELY. That way, when a cancellation happens, you don't waste 45 minutes looking for a YouTube tutorial—you just dive in and own the hour.

Your time is valuable.
And if you've been in real estate longer than 30 seconds, you've probably already experienced that weird identity crisis where you feel like you're always working...but somehow also not doing enough.

💼 This is a personal business, you can't take it personally

This is why **The Contingency Plan** exists. It helps you:

Avoid the spiral of disappointment

Eliminate emotional decision-making

Reduce guilt (yes, even "all my kids ate this week was McDonald's" guilt)

Protect your momentum, even on a tough day

Because you're a person, yes—but you're also a business.
So GET TO BUSINESS!

✦ Bonus: Built-in Fuel for Your Future

The best part? Your Contingency Plan doesn't just fill the gap in your calendar—it fills your tank.

Every time you complete a task from your list during a no-show, you're building new skills, strengthening your systems, and increasing your confidence. That's a WIN, baby. And it adds up.

⬛ Final Word: Grit Over Ghosts

Let's recap:

People will flake.

Appointments will fall through.

Deals will die.

But you do not spiral!

You pivot. You plan. You proceed.

And that, my friend, is what separates the real estate dreamers from the real estate do-ers. So next time that "must-see-today" lead ghosts you, don't waste your energy wondering what went wrong.

Whip out **The Contingency Plan**.

Get to work. Learn something new. Strengthen your business.

And remind yourself: No time is wasted when you invest it wisely.

You set aside time to work. So work. 💪

Contingency PLAN

Most Agents believe everything is a real estate emergency because no one properly explained to them that real estate, by it's very nature, is a series of **TINY CATASTROPHES**. Why? Because the biggest variable is **PEOPLE**. People are all **DIFFERENT**. Remember, it's a personal business, but you can't take it **PERSONALLY**. Just be **PREPARED**. When you set time to work, **WORK**. This running list of skills you want to learn more about & how to **QUICKLY ACCESS** them will save you from spiraling in the event of a no-show & serves as your **SMART AGENT TIME** wish list. This year, remember: **NO GUILT, ONLY GAINS**.

#	SMART AGENT SKILL	WHERE TO FIND	HOW TO ACCESS	DATE COMPLETED
EX.	Showing time app	https://showingtimeplus.com/solutions/showings-and-offers/appointment-center/app	iPhone; name@email.com; pw: Dominate2024$	
1				
2				
3				
4				
5				
6				
7				
8				
9				
10				
11				
12				

✏️ Final Word: Let My Life's Work WORK For You.

My dream? It's never been to hand out shiny objects that collect dust on your desk. It's to equip you—really equip you—with the tools, systems, and support you need to turn your real estate business into something sustainable. I want you to love this business as much as I do.

Whether you're brand new or leveling up your business for the 10th time, my mission stays the same:
To help Agents, Team Leaders, and Brokerages to sell more real estate and have way more fun doing it.

Everything in this workbook? It's not theory. It's not fluff.
It's the same proven structure that's helped me and my **Nationwide Network of Exceptional Agents** become multi-million dollar producers—year after year.
✦ So yes—this really is my life's work.
And it's here to **WORK FOR YOU**.

If these Top 10 Tools got you inspired, let's keep the momentum going.
Here's how:

☞ Explore more systems, trainings, and real talk at:
🌐 www.YourMarketingMama.com
◼️ Go to Amazon to grab a copy of the **Smart Agent Daily Planner**
🎥 Tune in to my REAL Real Estate Show – **The Crazy Agent Dinner Party**
📲 And don't forget to follow me on social for tips, tools & the occasional dance break💃

"Because Real Estate IS Crazy...AND You Don't Have To Be."
Let's build something amazing together. 🖤

✌️🖤🏠, AMANDA, *The Marketing Mama*
◼️ info@yourmarketingmama.com
📱 855.4YO.MAMA (text me!)
🔗 www.YourMarketingMama.com
📲 @YoMarketingMama | @YourMarketingMama
See you soon, Real Estate Do-er.

Made in United States
Orlando, FL
31 May 2025